Original Images
selected photographs

Joseph Fleming

Joseph Fleming

Colorblind Black & White
photography portfolio

Decades of being around accomplished talent producing absolutely phenomenal quality work has taught that we are capable of greatness. It is possible to meet our destiny and become it. Experiencing excellence done with such apparent ease and humble selfless gratification is the motivation for this photography. Most important was having the freedom

Being colorblind gives an advantage when composing black & white... less confusion.
This special collection selected from thousands of captures. All images were framed
in the camera and presented without edits, genuine as seen through the lens.
RAW conversion applied by proprietary panchromatic process.

Fine art prints from source files. Contact for custom work.

info@ BEACHNOISE.com

0351

0780

0826

1581

1608

2180

2467

3151

3359

3720

4035

4070

4099

4193

4533

5492

5750

5811

5846

6095

7182

8407

8470

8889

9024

9430

9970

9975

9980

10002